101
HUNTER/JUMPER TIPS

101 Essentials for Riding on the Flat and over Fences
HUNTER/JUMPER TIPS

Jessie Shiers

The Lyons Press
Guilford, Connecticut

An imprint of the Globe Pequot Press

Copyright © 2005 by The Lyons Press

The Lyons Press is an imprint of The Globe Pequot Press

10 9 8 7 6 5 4 3 2

Printed in the United States of America

Designed by Sheryl P. Kober

Photos by Jason and Jessie Shiers unless otherwise noted

Library of Congress Cataloging-in-Publication Data

Shiers, Jessie.
    101 hunter/jumper tips : essentials for riding on the flat and over fences / Jessie Shiers.
        p. cm.
    Includes bibliographical references and index.
    ISBN 978-1-59228-832-8 (trade pbk.)
    1. Hunt riding. 2. Jumping (Horsemanship) 3. Show jumpers (Horses)—Training. I. Title: One hundred one hunter/jumper tips. II. Title.

SF295.65.S55 2005
798.2'5—dc22

                                        2005044467

Contents

Introduction

unter/jumper is a phrase used to describe a unique world of training, riding, and showing horses and ponies. There are three distinct disciplines under the hunter/jumper umbrella: hunters, equitation, and jumpers.

The hunter division is judged subjectively on the horse's manners, style, and suitability. Hunters must be quiet, willing, and stylish movers. They are trained to carry themselves in a long and low frame and should be balanced under saddle, with little excess knee and hock action. Over fences, hunters should meet the jumps at an appropriate distance (taking off neither too far from nor too close to the fence), demonstrate a good *bascule* (rounding of the topline over the arc of the jump), have tidy front legs and square knees in the air, and finish crisply behind. They should be able to negotiate a course quietly and smoothly without too much interference from the rider. Hunters are also judged in under-saddle classes (also called *hack* or *flat* classes), meaning that there are no jumps.

The equitation division subjectively judges the rider's position, balance, and effectiveness of the aids on the flat and over fences. Equitation courses tend to be more complicated than hunter courses because they are designed to challenge the riders. Good equitation horses must be well trained, responsive to the rider's aids, steady to the jumps, and tend to jump with a flatter style that helps the rider maintain her position in the air.

The jumper division is judged objectively on *power and speed* using a point system. Rules for the various jumper classes can be complicated, but in a nutshell, horses must negotiate a course of jumps, and whoever finishes the round *clean*—that is, with no knock-downs, refusals, or falls—and with the fastest time wins. Style and form of the horse and rider are not considered, and there are no flat classes in the jumpers. Courses are generally built with bigger fences and more complicated turns and combinations than hunter or equi-tation courses. Many people consider the hunter and especially the equitation divisions to be preparation for junior riders who plan to one day compete in the jumpers.

Hunter/jumper shows can be found at all levels—from small, casual, one-day local schooling shows to big, weeklong national AA-rated shows.

In this book, you'll find tidbits of advice that apply to all three di-visions, at any level. Many of the tips are written with novice riders in mind, but others will be useful ideas for the more experienced ama-teur or professional. Whether you are heading to your first schooling show on your favorite lesson pony, retraining your off-the-track Thoroughbred as a jumper, or preparing a client's equitation horse for an upcoming Medal class, there will be a tip in this book for you.

The best piece of advice I've ever heard came from top trainer Judy Richter, who said that we have a duty to become the best riders we can be *because the horses deserve it.* They give us their best and try their hardest even when we ask for the impossible. We owe it to them to improve our skills as riders so that we can make their jobs fun and rewarding. Remember that we are participating in this sport because we love horses. If the ribbons are becoming more important than your horse's welfare, then take a step back and reassess your priorities. If you and your horse are not having fun, something is missing. So take a deep breath, give your horse a kiss, and enjoy your ride!

"There is something about **jumping** a horse over a fence, something that makes you **feel good**. Perhaps it is the risk, the gamble. In any event, it's a thing I need."

—William Faulkner

The horse is a sensitive creature. To protect his mouth, start beginning riders on the longe line before allowing them to pick up the reins.

tip 1. Ride without reins.

Ideally, every beginning rider should start her riding career on the longe line. New students at the Spanish Riding School in Vienna ride only on the longe line without stirrups or reins for their first six months. Without reins to hang onto for balance, you have no choice but to use your seat and legs, thereby developing the foundation of good riding position. More experienced riders, too, can benefit greatly from a little "reminder" lesson on the longe line. Using only your seat and leg aids, can you ask your horse to transition from a trot to a walk? How about a halt? Can you extend or collect his stride?

Jumping without reins requires balance and confidence.

tip 2. Jump without reins. For this confidence-

boosting exercise, a well-trained, dependable horse or pony is a prerequisite. Set up a simple gymnastic line. Start with a ground pole, then add a no-stride bounce to a crossrail, a one-stride to a small vertical—and if you're feeling brave, two strides to an oxer. In theory, once you've "plugged in" to such a combination, you don't need to steer; the horse should just canter straight through the line to the end. When you're ready to begin, tie your reins in a knot at the horse's withers. So tied, they're available for guidance before and after the gymnastic line, but they're also safely out of the way of your horse's front legs as he jumps.

Pick up a nice, active canter, head for your line, and just before the ground pole, drop your reins and put your hands on your hips. You'll be amazed at how aware you become of everything *but* your hands: your eyes, back, shoulders, legs, and heels all become so much more important without reins for security. Fine-tune this exercise by varying your arm position according to what your jumping flaws tend to be. If you often jump ahead, hold your arms straight out behind you. If you're a ducker, hold them out to the sides. If you roll your shoulders forward, then cross your arms behind your back to keep your chest open. If you tend to get left behind, keep your hands on your hips or in normal position as if you were still holding the reins.

After only two of sessions of practice, I was able to canter the line, turn, and halt, all without my reins—a great feeling of accomplishment.

Bonus tip: Not only is this exercise beneficial for your confidence and position, but it is also a useful preliminary to moving from the crest release to the automatic release (see tip 67 for a photo of an automatic release), since it helps you become independent of your hands and your horse's neck for support.

---

tip 3.

Riding without stirrups is one of the best ways to improve your seat and leg position, strength, and balance. Start with five or ten minutes during every ride, and work up to twenty or thirty minutes as your strength improves. After you warm up, cross your stirrups over the horse's withers so they don't bang his sides as he moves (see tip 4 for the best method). If your legs are weak so that you find posting the trot too difficult at first, riding a lot of transitions between halt, walk, and sitting trot will develop your strength and balance without killing you.

Don't torture yourself by practicing for too long. If you're in pain, your position will suffer, defeating the purpose of the exercise. Set yourself a small goal, such as posting the trot twice around the arena without stopping; then walk for several steps, reverse, and trot the other way. Before long you'll be able to post, ride in half-seat for a few strides, and canter, all without the support of stirrups. Eventually, riding without stirrups will feel the same as riding with them. That's when you know your riding has improved.

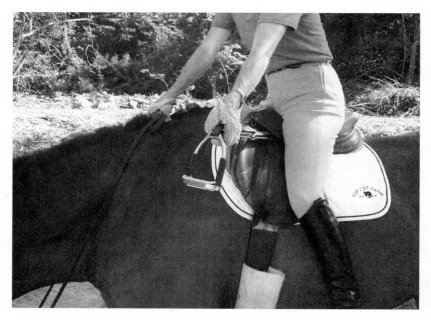

Pull the buckle away from the stirrup bar and forward before crossing the leather over the horse's withers.

tip 4.

When riding without stirrups, it's best to either remove them completely or cross them over the horse's withers so they won't bang the horse's sides and your ankles. Crossing the stirrups can result in an uncomfortable lump under your thigh if you don't take the time to do it correctly. To cross your stirrups, first pull the tail of the leather out of its keeper on the saddle flap. Then pull the buckle of the leather straight down away from the stirrup bar, so that there are 6 inches of leather between the buckle and the bar. Hold the leather flat against the saddle as you bring the stirrup forward, and then settle it down across the withers. Repeat on the opposite side.

In a horse show, an equitation judge should allow competitors sufficient time to cross the stirrups correctly when she asks for a test without stirrups.

Look, Ma—no stirrups!

tip 5.

If you can comfortably walk, trot, and canter and ride in your half-seat for several strides, all without stirrups, and you are jumping small courses, it's time to try jumping without stirrups. Cross your stirrups over the withers (see the preceding tip) or remove them from the saddle. Set up a simple, non-threatening crossrail, and be sure that you're working with an honest horse that won't run out or stop. Then just trot the jump. Don't ride any differently from the way you normally do; try to forget that you don't have stirrups. You'll be surprised at how easy this is. Trot and canter the crossrail both ways until you're comfortable. In your next session, try something higher.

This exercise benefits your leg position and security and is a great confidence booster. If you know you can jump without stirrups, then jumping with them is easy. On two occasions, I've been riding in a show and lost a stirrup (once when the horse stumbled, and once when my boots were slippery with rain), couldn't get it back in time, and had to finish the course with only one. I didn't pin in either case, but I finished my rounds safely and confidently with my dignity intact.

Every horse has something to teach you.

tip 6.

Ride different horses. If you own your own horse, you can easily slip into bad habits that he has taught you. For example, if he always hangs on the left rein, then it's likely that you also hang on the left rein. In addition, you've become accustomed to the length of his stride and the cadence of his trot. You know his every quirk—and you can bet he knows yours as well.

The best way to freshen up your riding and remind yourself of the basics is to ride a different horse. After months of the "same old, same old," you will be amazed at what a new horse can show you. While this tip applies to anyone who always rides the same horse, it is especially prescient for the owner of a green horse. Ride a finished horse, and you'll be astonished to recall what a horse's response to a half-halt is *supposed* to feel like.

If you are an equitation rider, you may be asked at a show to test on an unfamiliar horse. Practicing on various horses at home, especially unfamiliar ones, will help prepare you for this difficult test.

tip 7.

A great cure for jumping ahead or for riders who can't get the hang of distances is to jump with your eyes closed. It has many benefits. It will teach you to feel the distances rather than see them, to wait for your horse's jump to close your hip angle, and to trust your horse. For obvious reasons, this exercise can be dangerous and should only be attempted in the presence of an instructor and over fences that are 2 feet or lower. One final caveat: Make sure you have a horse you can trust! Don't try this on one that stops, spooks, or runs out.

Ride toward the fence in two-point position, and three strides out, close your eyes and grab mane. Just keep your leg on and wait for the fence. Savor the feeling of the horse moving under you, gathering his hind legs under him in that final stride, and taking you up and over the fence. If you've prepared correctly, the jump will close your hip and knee angles automatically and you won't need to make any "big moves" in front of the fence. Try this a few times, and then go back to jumping normally. Your distances will come much more naturally, and you won't be tempted to look down at the fence or jump ahead.

tip 8. To strengthen and test your position,

practice transitions at all gaits while in your two-point position. Walk to trot, trot to canter, canter to trot, canter to walk, walk to canter . . . even incorporate an occasional halt from any gait. If you have trouble maintaining your position through the transitions, you need to work on deepening your heel and balancing your weight over your horse's center of gravity. If you find yourself falling forward in the downward transitions, you may be gripping too much with your knees and creating a pivot point. Concentrate on distributing the contact evenly from your calf up through your inner thigh. If you fall back into the saddle, your legs are probably slipping forward. First, try shortening your stirrups a hole or two. If you still fall back, focus on keeping your heels deep and directly below your center of gravity. The more you practice this exercise, the easier it will become. And remember, there's no shame in grabbing mane!

When riding without stirrups, your leg position remains unchanged.

tip 9.

"If you find yourself bouncing at any gait," Anne Kursinski tells us, "there is stiffness somewhere in your joints—and when you're stiff, you're blocking out whatever message your horse is sending to you." The sitting trot makes many riders tense up in an effort to survive the jarring motion. This is counterproductive and actually makes bouncing much worse. Relaxing your seat and allowing it to naturally follow the motion of the horse's gait will produce a smooth, pleasant sitting trot.

Practice the sitting trot without stirrups to develop the feeling of the deep, soft seat that you need for this gait. If you start to bounce again upon taking up your stirrups, Kursinski counsels, "remind yourself to breathe, relax, follow, and 'feel.'"

Looking down at my hands has caused a chain reaction: My shoulders are rounded, my seat is shifted toward the pommel, and my lower leg has slipped back.

tip 10.

The horse will follow your eyes. If you stare at the jump, you'll get *to* it—but not over it. Worse, if you stare at the ground, you may well end up there if the horse chips or stops. Look at the jump to find your distance, and then look above and beyond it; you'll go where you're looking—over and beyond it—which is one of the reasons why keeping your eyes up is so important.

Another reason is that, as the character Ray sweetly informed us in the movie *Jerry Maguire*, "The human head weighs eight pounds." If you look down, you're dropping those eight pounds, plus some of the weight of your shoulders, directly where you don't want it to be—on the horse's forehand. Keeping your head up and eyes forward helps keep your body—and hence, the horse's body—well balanced.

tip 11.

Let's face it: not every horse is a naturally stylish and smooth jumper. Some horses compress their bodies at the base of the jump and then launch vertically. Others may drop their heads to look at the top rail just before jumping. Some horses kick out their hind legs upon landing. Some hunters with excellent style have a powerful, thrusty bascule that tends to launch their riders. These awkward jumping styles can be hard to ride. If you often find yourself getting "jumped out of the tack," left behind, or otherwise unseated, watch your horse from the ground to observe his particular jumping rhythm and style so you can be prepared when in the saddle. Set up a simple free-jumping chute by placing poles on either side of a jump and free-longe your horse over it repeatedly. Ingrain the flow in your mind like a videotape. Later, while riding, replay the tape mentally as you approach a jump. Your mental videotape will show you how your horse's body is moving through his takeoff, arc, and landing, helping you stay with him easily and quietly.

tip 12.

The key to riding with soft, quiet hands is not, in fact, in the hands themselves. Relaxing your fingers in an effort to achieve soft hands only allows the reins to slip and your communication with the horse to become muddled. Instead, think of softening and relaxing your entire arm, including the wrist and elbow, and especially the shoulder. In striving for the optimum equitation position, we often tense our back and shoulder muscles, trying to pull them into place. If your shoulders are tense, your elbows, wrists, and hands will carry this tension all the way through the reins to the horse's mouth. Instead, open and expand your chest while allowing your shoulders to relax naturally into place.

While at the halt and with a loose rein, repeatedly rotate your shoulders in small circles—up, back, and down—while keeping them soft and relaxed. Allow the motion instigated by your shoulders to transmit itself down to your elbows and wrists, so they gently follow the circles as well. Remember this feeling when you take up a light contact and trot off. And don't forget to breathe.

While exhaling, think of the feeling of relaxing your shoulders loosely down and back, allowing the softness to follow your arms to the reins. You'll instantly recognize the feeling of "soft hands" that you've been trying to achieve. Your horse, who will feel it too, will relax and soften in response.

tip 13.

Stretch before riding. While allowing your horse to warm up by walking on a loose rein, lift your arms straight out at shoulder height, forming a T-shape. Turn to the left and drop your left hand onto your horse's rump, bending your spine. Keeping your chest open and eyes up, stretch your right arm up and over your head. Let your left elbow bend and straighten to absorb the motion of the horse's walk. Settle into the stretch for thirty seconds, then sit back up, rotate to the right, and perform the stretch in the opposite direction. This motion will loosen your shoulder joint and open your rib cage, allowing you to use your upper body and shoulders independently of your hips and seat later in the ride.

Next, assume two-point position, sinking your heel down and closing your lower leg around the horse. Make the T with your arms again, and, being careful to keep weight in your left leg, rotate to the right and reach down to touch your right toe with your left hand (or at least *try* to touch the toe!). Again, repeat this stretch on the opposite side. You'll feel it in your lower back, hamstrings, calves, and heels.

The hip flexor stretch. Lean forward slowly until you feel the stretch.

tip 14.

Stretching after a ride is equally important to prevent sore muscles. Here are a few good stretches for riders to practice at home each night while watching TV.

Sit on the floor with your legs spread in front of you. Lean over first one leg and then the other, stretching the hamstring. Don't point your toe—instead, flex your ankle the way you do when on a horse.

While still sitting, bring your feet together, forming a diamond shape with your legs. Lean forward to stretch your groin muscles.

Stand up, spread your feet apart, and bend your left knee, shifting your weight onto that side. Keep the right foot in contact with the floor to stretch your right inner thigh. Repeat on the other side.

To stretch your hip flexor, balance on your left foot and bring your right foot up to rest the back of the foot on the front of your left thigh, as high up toward your crotch as your right knee's flexibility allows. Bend the left knee slightly and lean forward until you feel the stretch along the front of your right hip. Repeat on the other side.

The classic ankle and hamstring stretch for riders who have trouble keeping their heels down is to stand on the edge of a step or stair on the balls of your feet, as if the step were a stirrup, and sink your body weight down into your heels.

This photo shows the first beat of the left lead canter stride—the "one" moment, in which Teddy's right hind is on the ground. If Marty had applied the aids for a lead change with her left leg, Teddy would have stepped down with his left hind instead of his right hind, landing on the right lead.

tip 15.

Timing is of the essence when applying the aids. This fact is perhaps nowhere more clear than in the flying change of lead, for which you must ask at the precise moment that the horse's four legs are off the ground—that is, the moment of suspension. This is the moment when, to use the left lead as an example, the horse is about to step down with his right hind leg for the first beat of the left lead canter stride. When you ask for the change to the right lead during the moment of suspension by applying your left leg behind the girth, the horse is able to respond correctly by stepping down with his left hind instead of the right hind, thus landing on the right lead. One of the reasons why it is easier to teach a green horse to change his leads over a ground pole is that the pole increases the amount of time spent in suspension, making it obvious to both the rider and the horse just when that precise moment occurs.

To find the moment of suspension without using a ground pole, Anna Jane White-Mullin describes a simple technique in her book, *Winning*: "It helps if you silently count the footfalls a few strides before the change: 'one, two, three . . . one, two, three . . . one, two, three . . .'" The slight pause after each *three* and before the next *one* is the moment of suspension.

tip 16.

Many riders are consistently unbalanced and tend to place more weight in one stirrup than the other. Some clues that you may carry more weight in, for example, the left stirrup are that you may often lose the right stirrup at the canter; your horse falls in off the rail when tracking left; and your instructor tells you that you're collapsing your right hip. To remedy this problem, try dropping the left stirrup altogether. Keep the right stirrup. Walk, trot, and canter with only the right stirrup. Ride this way for a few days, and then take back the left stirrup. You'll be cured!

tip 17. Don't pick at your horse on the approach to a fence, trying to find the perfect distance. Instead of trying to whittle the horse's stride into the right spot by half-halting here and there or giving a cluck or some leg now and then, establish a forward, bouncy canter and then wait until you see a distance, four or five strides out. Then make one adjustment, if necessary. If the spot looks long, then send the horse forward. If it looks tight, then sit up and half-halt firmly. Make this one adjustment really count, so you can do it once and then wait for the fence.

Bonus tip: When turning before the approach to a jump, keep control of the horse's outside shoulder and hip with your outside rein and leg. If the horse is bulging through the turn, it will throw your eye off and you won't be able to see the distance accurately.

Resistance in the form of tiny half-halts through your leg and seat will shorten the horse's stride. Notice the long rein—the hands are not restricting the stride.

A following seat, allowing hands, and encouraging legs result in a lengthened stride compared to the previous photo.

tip 18.

Riders' attempts to lengthen a horse's stride often result in a faster pace with quicker steps, but the actual length of the stride remains the same. This happens when we ask with our legs for more speed, while not allowing the stride to extend with our seat and body. While working on the flat, practice using only your seat to lengthen and shorten your horse's stride at the walk. Begin by walking on contact on a 20-meter circle with no stirrups. As the horse walks, feel the muscles and bones of your seat as they follow the motion of his back. Notice the way your lower back moves to allow this following seat. Now ask the horse to shorten his stride, not by pulling on the reins but by stilling the movement of your seat with each stride. Resist the horse's forward movement by momentarily tightening and then releasing your seat and lower back muscles. With each stride, think "whoa . . . whoa . . . whoa." You should be able to feel the horse's stride become shorter. Now relax and let your seat follow again, and think of the horse's stride becoming longer and longer. Practice changing from long strides to short strides and back until you have it down.

The same principle applies at the canter. To shorten stride, rather than hauling on the reins, resist upward through your seat and back with each stride. To lengthen, soften your lower back and allow your seat to follow the motion of the horse's body while you give the reins forward just a bit to allow the horse to use his neck. On a green or resistant horse, you may need to support your seat aids with rein contact to shorten and with leg to lengthen, but the foundation of stride control is always the seat.

tip 19.

If you tend to anticipate, tense up, and stop breathing as you approach a fence, help yourself to relax and breathe by singing. It is impossible to not breathe while singing. Moreover, the analytical side of your brain will be occupied with remembering the lyrics, which frees your body to relax and follow the horse without hindrance. A children's song, such as "The Alphabet Song" or "Mary Had a Little Lamb," adds an element of silliness and playfulness that will help you relax further and make jumping seem like a game rather than a difficult task. An added benefit is that with repetition, the cadence of the song can help you balance the rhythm of your horse's stride.

Melissa is asking Gabby to back correctly by using her leg and seat.
Observe the gentle rein contact and the quiet obedience of the pony.

tip 20.

Despite the phrase *rein back*, the correct way to back a horse is not by pulling the reins. Backing is a movement, and using the reins to pull back is a cue to the horse to stop moving. Pulling or sawing at the horse's mouth may eventually cause him to back up to escape the uncomfortable bit pressure, but it will not be a pretty picture. He'll be unhappy and will show it with pinned ears, hollow back, nose in the air, and swishing tail. Instead, ask a horse to back by first slightly lightening your seat to allow his back to round and his hind legs to step under his body. Then apply the forward aids, but maintain rein contact to block the horse from moving forward. Since he can't step forward but you are asking him to move, the logical response is to step backward.

tip 21.

The half-halt is possibly the most necessary aid for advanced riders and the least well understood aid for novice riders. Half-halts are used to prepare the horse for a transition or change of bend, to steady a quick horse or engage a dull one, to set up for a jump, and otherwise call the horse's mind to attention and bring his body into balance. The half-halt rebalances the horse's weight over his hindquarters, engages his hocks by creating impulsion that drives them farther under his body, and lightens and elevates his front end.

For a novice rider or a green horse, the most straightforward way to achieve a half-halt is to apply the driving leg aids and restraining rein aids nearly simultaneously. The leg aid should precede the rein aid by a split second. The horse's hind legs are thereby driven forward and the resulting increase in pace is restricted by contact with the horse's mouth. (This is what is meant by riding *leg to hand* or riding a horse *up to the bit*.) Since the energy generated by the hind legs can't go forward, it must be channeled upward in the form of increased impulsion and lightness of the forehand. More advanced riders on sensitive, well-trained horses are capable of performing a half-halt mainly through the action of the seat and legs, using them simultaneously as a driving and restraining aid.

tip 22.

All riders should know how to use the pulley rein in case of emergency. This is a very strong, even harsh, rein aid that is not to be used unless absolutely necessary—that is, on a horse that is bolting. For safety, children should be taught the pulley rein early in their pony-riding careers.

Falling from a galloping horse is extremely unsafe, so your first concern should be to regain your own balance if you have lost it. This is generally most easily accomplished by assuming two-point position (unless the horse is actively trying to pull you out of the saddle with the reins, in which case you must immediately sit firmly in the saddle). Once you have organized yourself and shortened your reins, sit down into a solid three-point position and apply the pulley rein. Anchor your weaker hand (usually the left hand if you're right-handed) on the horse's withers, grabbing mane if necessary. Use your other hand to pull up and back with all your strength until the horse slows or stops. This action creates a pulley effect on the horse's mouth with the bit that is extremely severe, but can save you from a wreck.

Bonus tip: If a bolt happens in an arena or other enclosed area, anchor your inside hand and use the outside hand as your pulley rein. This has the benefit of forcing the horse's nose toward the rail so he'll have to stop to avoid crashing into it.

tip 23.

It's been said a thousand times, but I'll say it again: Breathe! For many reasons—tension, concentration, nervousness, even fear—riders literally forget to breathe while riding. This doesn't mean that they hold their breath (or we'd see a lot more riders passing out). It means that they forget to breathe *correctly*. They take short, shallow breaths that allow tension to remain in the abdomen. Sensitive horses feel this tension and become tense themselves.

The correct way to breathe is to inhale deeply into your belly. Imagine that your diaphragm—the flat muscle under your lungs—is dropping down toward your pelvis as you inhale. Your shoulders should not rise. As you exhale, allow all the air to ease out of your lungs. Don't force it out. Practice this by lying on your back with a hand resting on your stomach. If you are breathing correctly, your hand will rise as you inhale and drop as you exhale. Incorrect breathing has the opposite effect.

Next time you're riding, remember this breathing technique. A good, solid exhale helps your horse relax and remember to breathe himself. Often when I am asking my horse to do something new or challenging, we both forget to breathe. When he becomes tense and upset, with a high head and hollow back, I exhale audibly—like a big sigh—letting him hear me. Invariably, his response is to sigh deeply, relax, and drop his head.

When asking for a downward transition, inhale as you resist the horse's forward motion, and exhale as you release the horse into the new gait. Believe it or not, this even works when longeing a horse if he is in tune with you. On several occasions, I have watched my horse trot merrily around the round pen, ignoring my every command to "whoa" or "walk." Then I remember the magic of breathing. I take a deep breath into my belly, and let it out in an audible sigh, letting go of all tension and expectation. The horse walks.

If you've attended to steps 1, 2, and 3, the jump will take care of itself.

tip 24.

Trainer and sports psychologist Kip Rosenthal has broken down the process of riding a course into four steps: As you approach each line, establish your canter, establish your track, monitor your pace and track, and jump the fence. Then repeat this sequence at the next line.

1   Establish your canter. Make it a pace that allows options; your horse should be in front of your leg in case you must move up, but not so much in your hand that you'd have trouble steadying if required.

2   Establish your track. If you're heading for a line that has two fences, look for the first fence but don't turn until you can see the center of the second fence between the first fence's standards. If it's a line with a single fence, find a point at the end of the ring that you want to ride to and wait to turn until you see that point between the standards of the first fence. This method will ensure a straight track to the fence, rather than an angled or curving track.

3 Monitor your pace and track. More often than not, you won't have to do anything at all. Make no adjustments unless and until necessary. Unless the horse makes an error, such as slipping behind your leg or deviating from the track that you established to the fence, force yourself to do nothing; if you've gotten this far, the distance will work out. How do you know? The fence will "tell" you what to do, such as whether to move up or to steady. Trust the fence—and yourself.

4 Jump the fence. Then ride out your line and go back to step 1 as you head for the next line of fences.

"As he knotted the reins and took his stand the horse's soul came into his hand, and up from the mouth that held the steel came an innermost word, half thought, half feel."

—John Masefield

If he'll jump a dog, he'll jump anything!

tip 25. Jump strange objects. Your horse

is likely to spook at every unusual fence he encounters at a show if at home he jumps nothing but the painted poles your instructor uses for lessons. If you're like the rest of us and you'd really rather your horse go over the fences with you, condition him to expect the unexpected whenever he's jumping. Anything lying around the barn will do, as long as safety is taken into consideration. For example, trash barrels, painted car tires, stuffed animals, plastic tarps, a horizontal Christmas tree . . . The list goes on.

I have heard of horses who were taught to jump over the stream of water from a fire hose. Objects that move or make noise in the wind—such as streamers, pinwheels, and wind chimes—are especially scary. You can be equally creative with standards and wings. The funkiest jump I ever saw used two fiberglass statues of the Blues Brothers as wings.

Bonus tip: To make a simple liverpool for schooling at home, buy a long, plastic winter sled, lay it lengthwise under a vertical, and fill it with water.

When leg-yielding, the horse's body is bent slightly away from the direction of travel. Note that the horse's hindquarters directly follow his shoulders, rather than being left behind as the shoulders lead.

tip 26.

Use the leg-yield each time you ride to "tune the horse in" to your leg and seat aids. As you're walking to warm up, turn down the centerline and ask for a very slight left bend through the horse's body. Each time you feel his left hind leg stepping forward under his body, squeeze with your left leg to ask that left hind to move sideways. Keep a feel of the outside (right) rein both to keep your horse from falling out over his outside shoulder and to prevent him from overflexing to the left. If he ignores you, wake him up with a tap of your crop at the same moment you apply your leg. Try this exercise in both directions, first at the walk and then at the trot. It teaches the horse that *leg* can mean *sideways*, which will be necessary to keep him straight to the jumps.

A good trainer teaches a horse that he has to jump, even if a rider gets him to a tight spot.

tip 27.

Trainers should ride a horse the way his owner rides him. A friend of mine was once at a big show watching noted trainer Geoff Teall schooling an amateur's horse. Teall looked unusually sloppy and loose in the saddle. My friend turned to a knowledgeable acquaintance and wondered aloud, "What's wrong with Geoff today? He's a much better rider than that."

His acquaintance responded, "Oh yes, of course he is. He's riding like that on purpose because that's how the horse's owner rides." Teall was teaching the horse that he needed to do his job, even if the rider wasn't doing hers so well.

Longeing is a good way to develop respect and obedience in a young horse. (Courtesy of Sarah Weingarten)

tip 28.
All horses should be taught how to longe safely and obediently. Longeing is useful in several ways: It teaches the horse to respect his trainer. It is a way to teach the horse verbal commands that can come in handy in a pinch when riding. Longeing in side reins teaches the horse to accept the bit and carry himself in a frame. It is a good way to exercise a horse when you're unable to ride for any reason. And it's a safe way to take the edge off a horse when he's too fresh to ride at home or at a show.

If you don't know how to longe a horse, ask your trainer to teach you. Most horses these days know how, since most modern training methods begin with longeing as a preliminary to riding. If your horse does not know how to longe—if he is an off-the-track racehorse, for example—start off in a round pen, which keeps him contained and focused on you. Lacking a round pen, ask a helper to lead the horse on the circle, walking beside his outside shoulder for his first few longe lessons. This helps the horse grasp the basic concept of longeing: working in a circle.

Trail riding in open country with company is an excellent refresher for body and soul.

tip 29.

Trail riding—how do I love thee? Let me count the ways: It breaks up the monotony of ring work for both you and your horse. It strengthens the bond between the two of you as you forge new paths together. It increases your confidence and his. It improves your seat and your balance as you follow his movement up and down hills and around rocks and trees. It forces you to practice your half-seat as you gallop. It allows your horse to stretch and move without the confines of corners and bending lines. It gets you out into the fresh country air. It conditions him. It helps his agility, surefootedness, and balance, as he must navigate over uneven terrain. It strengthens his hindquarters as he climbs and descends the hills. It exposes and desensitizes him to many new things—deer, bicycles, hikers with backpacks, puddles, strange-looking rocks.

Take every opportunity to go out on the trail, even if it means trailering to an appropriate place.

tip 30.

Head for the hills. Hill work is great for the horse's overall fitness. Powering up the hills and balancing down them strengthens the horse's back, hindquarters, and stifles—all the muscles used for impulsion, collection, and jumping. After your ring work, leave the arena and find a small slope that you can walk up and down for five minutes. When traveling both uphill and downhill, assume a two-point position and keep your weight in your heels to allow the horse free use of his back. When going downhill, lengthen your reins so the horse can use his neck for balance. Use your legs to keep the horse straight, because going down a hill at an angle can be dangerous on slippery or steep terrain; it's easy for the horse to lose his footing and slip sideways, possibly falling on your leg or injuring himself. Work up to steeper and longer hills, eventually up to thirty minutes at a time.

Bonus tip: Your horse may want to gallop up the steeper hills. It's actually easier for him, because he can push off forcefully with both hind legs. It's fine to allow him to gallop a few times for fun, but encourage him to walk and trot the hills as well, to strengthen his muscles more effectively.

Big, strong, green horses may brace against your aids and "blow through" a half-halt. When this happens, halt the horse.

tip 31.

When riding a strong, green horse who ignores your every attempt at a half-halt, remember that if you can stop your horse, you can slow him down. As he becomes faster and more strung out at the trot, use a half-halt (see tip 21) to ask him to rebalance and slow down. When he ignores you, shut him down—halt immediately, and I mean HALT! Pause and praise him for stopping, then trot off and try your half-halt again. If he still isn't listening, halt again. Gradually, change from bringing him to a full halt to bringing him to an almost-but-not-quite halt—and then trot off instantly. This sequence will set him back on his hocks and rebalance him just like a true half-halt, even though it's much more visible and more abrupt than we'd prefer.

As the horse begins to respond to you more promptly and obediently, you can soften and lighten your aids, eventually asking him just to hesitate and balance himself over his hocks without the big, obvious change in stride and pace.

Bonus tip: For a horse that's very strong or heavy on his forehand, after the halt, rein back for four steps before immediately trotting off.

Sal calls out the next fence for Marty as she jumps.

tip 32.

Many horses tend to gallop through lines and rush single fences. Once they know which fence the rider is heading for, they're off to the races. If your horse is one of these freight trains, try this fun activity to keep him guessing. Set up an interesting variety of different jumps in a large arena, in such a way that you could jump them in any number of combinations (not just side-diagonal-side-diagonal). Ask a friend or your instructor to stand in the ring and call out which fence she wants you to jump next, one at a time. Ask her to get creative with unusual lines and changes of gait, such as "Turn right and jump the green oxer!" or, "Trot, roll back, and jump the vertical again the other way!" I once had to halt, back up, and turn on the haunches, then canter two strides to a skinny. If you don't know what's coming, neither can your horse, so he won't be able to anticipate. This is a fabulous exercise for setting your horse back and really making him listen to you. Once he realizes what you're doing, he'll love the game as much as you do.

Courses at shows are often built with awkward striding to challenge you. Practice at home by shortening and lengthening stride.

tip 33.

To help make your horse more adjustable, vary the number of strides in a line. Set up an easy six (see tip 36), then try to ride it in five strides (lengthening) or seven strides (shortening). Depending on your horse's abilities, you can make the exercise more challenging by shortening and lengthening stride even more. Remember that hitting the right distance in a line is a result of the ride coming in to the line. If you're aiming to lengthen for the five, approach the first jump with more pace. Ride right to the base of the jump so your horse doesn't leave long and land too close to the fence so you have to make up the lost distance by really powering through the line. Conversely, if you're shooting for the quiet seven, come into the line with a collected canter. Remember, *collected* doesn't mean dull and flat—it means shorter strides with more impulsion.

This rider's head position shows that she's planning to turn right upon landing, and you can see by the horse's front legs that he has responded to her clear weight aids by preparing to land on the right lead.

tip 34.

Practice landing on the lead that you want, not the lead your horse chooses. Set up a simple one-stride on the centerline. Trot in and canter out, halting on a straight line after the fence. Do this three or four times until you're sure your horse is really listening to you and is waiting for the halt aids after the line.

The next time you jump the line, plan to land on the left lead. After the first jump in your line, look left and open your left rein just a hair, guarding with your left leg in case your horse sees the rein aid as an invitation to run out. As you jump, keep looking left and weight the outside (right) stirrup a little more than the inside one. That may be all the help your horse needs to land on the left lead. If so, continue on down the rail, drop back to a trot, and jump the line again, this time planning to land on the right lead.

If things don't go so well and your horse lands on the wrong lead, try again, being more definite with your weight and rein aids. Be sure to have him positioned a bit to the left in the middle of the line. Carry your left hand out and up a little to ask him to flex his neck to the left, freeing his right shoulder (but be careful not to pull him off balance).

The first combination in this line is a bounce; the second is a short one-stride.

tip 35.
Another exercise to develop adjustability is to begin with a line that you think is a perfect one-stride for your horse's step (see tip 36). Jump this line a few times, and then move the first fence 1 to 2 feet closer to the second fence. (If the horse is quite green, 6 inches closer is plenty.) Now you'll have to collect your horse and ride him right to the base of the fence. Don't treat this combination as a bounce (no strides between the fences); it should still be a one-stride line.

To practice lengthening, move the first fence back 1 to 2 feet from its original position. Don't let your horse chip in an extra stride; keep your leg on to make that awkward distance work.

tip 36. Measuring strides when building

a course involves many considerations, such as fence height, horse or pony size, footing, and variations in terrain. Good horse-show course designers are highly sought after for their ability to calculate precise distances. In general, however, the following rules may be applied when building schooling courses at home.

The distance between fences up to 2'6" for the average horse with a 12-foot stride is 6 feet for landing, plus 12 feet per stride, plus 6 feet for the takeoff spot. So a one-stride line is 24 feet, a two-stride line is 36 feet, a three-stride line is 48 feet, and a four-stride line is 60 feet.

As the fences are raised, the distances must lengthen to accommodate the increase in pace needed to clear the higher fences. As a rule of thumb, add 6 inches per stride for every 6 inches in fence height over 2'6". For example, a two-stride line over 3' fences must be 37 feet—1 foot longer than the 2'6" distance.

Distances for ponies are even more complex because they must take the pony's size into account. Some large ponies have nearly the equivalent of a 12-foot horse stride, while the smallest of small ponies may have a stride as short as 8 feet. In general, however, calculate average pony distances using a 10-foot stride, plus the same 6 feet for takeoff and 6 feet for landing (since the arc over a jump depends on the jump height, not the length of the pony's stride). Vary the distances by 6 inches to 1 foot per stride based on experience with your own pony.

Bonus tip: When setting a placing pole before or after a jump, remember that the pole must be farther out than the estimated 6-foot takeoff spot. The horse's feet must land between the pole and the fence, not *on* the pole. Place the pole 9 feet out for horses or large ponies, and 8 feet out for medium or small ponies.

Stretching the horse's head to each side improves lateral flexibility.
(Courtesy of Sarah Weingarten)

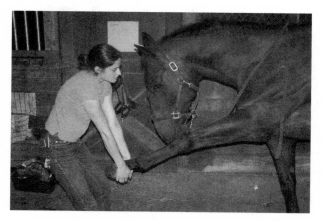

Stretching the horse's front legs improves mobility of the shoulder joint. Always unhook the cross ties in case the horse loses his balance.

tip 37. Stretch your horse. As part of your

grooming routine, hold a carrot near his shoulder to encourage him to stretch his neck and back as he reaches for it. Always stretch both sides. Finally, hold a third carrot between his forelegs to encourage him to reach down and stretch his topline. Be careful not to ask him to stretch too far; some horses are overly enthusiastic about grabbing the carrot and could fall down.

After saddling, stand in front of your horse, pick up his front leg, and slowly stretch it forward and up as far as it will go, without forcing it or pulling the horse off balance. Be sure to pull straight forward, holding the leg under the heels of the hoof—pulling at an angle will hurt. Gently move the leg in counterclockwise circles to loosen the shoulder joint. Make sure to stretch both legs equally. If the horse shows any sign of resistance or discomfort, you have stretched the leg too far; be more gentle next time. Most horses learn to enjoy stretching and will help you by extending the leg and pointing the toe as you pull.

tip 38.

To help a horse that likes to cut the turn after a jump at home or in the show ring, and to help you learn to reorganize more quickly after a fence, practice leg-yielding after each fence. Set two low fences (crossrails or 2' verticals) in a five-stride line on the quarter line of the arena (the quarter line is the length of the arena halfway between the centerline and the rail). Canter in and ride the line. As you land from the second fence, don't look left or right; keep your gaze focused on the end of the ring. Halt the horse smoothly on a straight line well before the end of the arena. Then leg-yield him four or five steps toward the rail (see tip 26). Halt again, and praise the horse. Then pick up the canter and re-peat. Be sure to practice this in both directions. With repetition, your horse will learn to wait for your aids after a line rather than rushing off and cutting the corner in his haste to get to the next fence.

tip 39.

Here's a great exercise to do in the winter when you're stuck in an indoor arena, because you don't need much space. Ride a figure eight over one jump, with the jump at the center of the 8. Vary the exercise by making the circles smaller or larger.

The figure-eight pattern is beneficial in many ways: You must ride precisely to get the horse straight to the jump from the bending lines of the figure eight. You have to get your leads. Without a placing pole or another jump to set you up, you must ride the fence *off your eye*, which helps you develop an ability to find distances without counting strides.

Gordon Wright, the legendary trainer of such greats as George Morris, Ronnie Mutch, and Bill Steinkraus, used to school his students over a single fence in a field for months. By the time they finished, they'd developed an eye for distances and a sense of track and pace.

Bonus tip: A correctly ridden figure eight consists of two circles with a straight segment at the point where they join, not two teardrop shapes connected at the intersection of diagonal lines.

---

tip 40.

Timing is key when using a crop to reinforce your leg aids. If you use the crop too often or too late, the horse will not understand its meaning. Squeeze with your leg first. Failing a response, ask again, a bit more firmly. This time, if the horse still ignores you, instantly use the crop to hit him once directly behind your leg. This sequence tells the horse, "If you ignore my soft aid, you'll get a smack." The horse should soon learn to avoid being smacked by responding promptly to your leg.

Some horses are very sensitive to the mere suggestion of the crop. Others seem to have sides of iron. If you use the crop correctly and get no response, don't just keep hitting the horse. Unable to associate his discomfort with your request for forward movement, he will not know why you are hitting him. Instead, relax your aids for a moment, and begin the sequence again— squeeze, *squeeze*, smack!—but this time, smack harder. You need to hit him hard enough that he feels it and jumps forward in surprise. When he does, praise him lavishly. He'll soon figure out that *leg* means *forward*, and if he ignores it, he'll be stung. By the same token, be sure to praise him when he moves forward from leg alone as well.

tip 41. There are several ways to train a horse to respond to the cluck, but the basic principle is to create the sound and then immediately send the horse strongly forward. Jane Savoie recommends finding a long, flat stretch where you can really ask the horse to gallop forward. At the top of the stretch, apply your leg. Failing a response, cluck once and immediately send the horse forward at a gallop using a crop or spurs briefly for impetus, if necessary. Several repetitions of this process will result in a horse that leaps forward at the sound of the cluck, expecting to be asked to gallop off. This kind of a response can save you from a sticky spot approaching a fence, *if* you save it for those key moments.

tip 42.

Don't overuse the cluck. If you're constantly clucking, your horse will eventually tune you out. Then when you find yourself in a situation where you really need that extra giddyup—for example, you're dying in the middle of an in-and-out— you'll cluck to your horse and get no response. To avoid this problem, first make sure that your horse is really trained to the cluck; then use it *only when you really mean it*. When you do cluck, only make the sound once, not several times in a row. Otherwise the horse will come to believe that "cluck cluck cluck" means forward, but "cluck" does not. The same goes for using the stick or spurs—only one appli- cation at a time, and only when you need them.

tip 43.
In his book *Basic Training of the Young Horse*, Reiner Klimke offers advice for at-home training of a horse who is apt to rush before or after fences. To teach the horse who rushes toward the fence, "put up several *cavalletti* [ground poles] in front of the fence," he advises. The cavalletti should be 3 to 4 feet apart, with 12 feet between the final cavalletti and the fence. "The horse is asked to trot over the cavalletti and it is left to him to decide whether he trots or canters over the fence. This is ridden in rising trot."

Klimke continues: "To help horses that are apt to rush off after jumping, one puts a second or even a third cavalletti behind the jump." These cavalletti should be placed at one stride (12-foot) intervals after the fence. "The attention of the horse will be focused on the cavalletti. Even when jumping, the horse will look down at the cavalletti in front of it and will also unconsciously round its back. It will not have time to run off and the rider can keep control."

tip 44.
Almost every horse will occasionally surprise his rider by refusing a fence—whether because of an awkward approach, a scary-looking fence, a physical problem in the horse, or, in the worst case, because the horse is what William Steinkraus calls a "dirty" refuser. Refusing is a dangerous, frightening, and unacceptable action and needs to be corrected immediately. "In the case of a refusal for whatever reason—even justifiable ones," Steinkraus relates in his *Reflections on Riding and Jumping*, "my first action is to spank the horse. Refusing is totally unacceptable behavior in a jumper under almost any circumstances, and it's important that the horse should understand this."

Jerking on the horse's mouth with the reins or hitting the horse on the shoulder, neck, or head is not only abusive, but it's also counterproductive. The punishment for a refusal should always encourage the horse to think and move *forward*. "Three or four good whacks on the rump should be plenty," says Steinkraus. "Then come back to the fence in perfect control, and do *not* change your riding. If horses will only jump for you when you're kicking and whipping, you're in deep trouble; they have to go when you're riding normally."

Bonus tip: "Whatever you do, don't make a big crest release or anticipate the next takeoff," Steinkraus warns. "All the congenital refusers, the 'dirty' refusers who have the idea always lurking in their minds, are just waiting for you to drop them so they can refuse."

tip 45. When working through a difficult moment with a horse or pony, it's important to take into consideration the personality of the individual horse. Top hunter trainer Judy Richter offers some advice on spooky ponies: "If he is a bully, then bully him. If he is honestly timid, then you need to coax him. If he is just spooky, you must be firm and reassuring. For example, if a blanket is slung over the railing of the riding ring, the bully takes advantage of the situation and spooks. He needs you to give him a smack and march him right up to it. The timid one or the spook needs to be firmly reassured and not forced to go right up to the fearsome object. Given a little space and a firm leg on his opposite side, most equines will gradually accept the scary blanket as they pass it often during the course of the ride."

It's harder for a horse to rush when he's bending.

tip 46.

When first beginning to work with a young, hot horse, it's important to establish a good rhythm and pace at the working trot. Attempting to forcibly hold in such a horse with restricting reins tends to bottle up the horse's energy—leading at best to a quick, choppy stride, and at worst to an explosive release of energy in the form of a buck, bolt, or rear.

Instead, contain the horse's forward impulsion by riding small circles, so that the horse does not have the opportunity to rush or break to a canter. A circle forces the horse to concentrate on the bend of his body, the placement of his feet, and the organization of his stride so he does not throw himself off balance. Each time the horse begins to rush, immediately ask him to trot a 10-meter circle. In the beginning, you may end up riding around the entire ring executing tiny circles, but eventually, the horse will learn to contain himself and respect your aids. As he settles, you'll use larger and less-frequent circles until it is possible to ride the horse straight at a balanced, calm working trot.

Include unusual jumps in your regular schooling, such as "skinny," airy fences like this one.

tip 47. When schooling a young horse

over fences, change the height, order, and arrangement of jumps frequently. Reiner Klimke writes in his book, *Basic Training of the Young Horse*, that "every change makes the horse more attentive, teaches it in time to look after itself and furthers the competence of horse and rider." An intelligent horse quickly becomes bored by repeating the same thing over and over, so a change of jumps will help to engage his attention. Repeatedly dismounting to move the jumps when working alone is time-consuming and awkward. Therefore, Klimke recommends having a helper on the ground to "move the jumps quickly and without fuss." A young or novice rider will often be willing to lend a hand in exchange for the educational experience of watching a more skilled rider train a horse.

Bonus tip: Klimke reminds us that "one should not hesitate to ask the helper frequently, even if he is not a qualified teacher, how the horse has jumped, what the seat of the rider was like, and so on." A ground person's eyes are an invaluable aid.

If you pick a fight with your horse, make sure you have the determination to handle the consequences and follow through. If the horse wins, he'll know he has the upper hand.

tip 48.

To convince a horse to respect your judgment, it's important to always come out on top in a difference of opinions. "I've always believed it's better to be proactive, to set up the situation so the pony does not fight back," Judy Richter says. "On the other hand, if you do need to win a fight, set it up so that you *can* win. Jump the spooky jump going toward the in gate or barn first if you are finessing the issue. Jump the jump away from the in gate if you want to pick a fight, but be armed with a whip, spurs, and lots of determination, so you outwit him and he does not outwit you." This is not an invitation to beat your horse; it's a reminder that riders need to be firm and forceful with difficult horses. If you do get angry and catch yourself using your whip and spurs for punishment rather than reinforcement of the leg aids, it's time to stop for a moment, walk on a loose rein, and take a deep breath. Once your emotions are under control, come back to the difficult exercise with renewed patience.

A horse that can spot his own distances will be able to help you out in the show ring.

tip 49.

Good hunter and jumper riders know the importance of *seeing a distance* to a fence and being able to ride the horse to it accurately. However, there is one situation in which it may be best *not* to seek a perfect distance: when riding a young or green horse. "In most cases," offers Anne Kursinski, "letting your horse figure out the distance himself is great for his education." If he learns not to rely on you, he'll be able to help you out and will someday become a safe mount for a green rider to learn on. In addition, a horse that finds some awkward distances and hits the jumps as a result will learn that hitting a jump stings, which will make him a much more careful jumper. "On the other hand," Anne continues, "if you manufacture every distance for him, he'll rely on you and stop trusting his own instincts. When you find yourself in a jump-off, where you have to go fast against the clock, or in a class where the jumps are bigger or more difficult than any you've faced before, you won't be able to ask him to help out. His sense of self-preservation will have withered away from disuse."

The horse should follow the contact by stretching down and forward. (I am being a bit casual here at the walk. At the trot, I would keep more rein contact.)

tip 50.

As a suppling and strengthening exercise, as a reward to the horse, and as a test to find out whether you've engaged his hind end and asked him to use himself correctly, allow the horse to stretch down and forward on contact at the end of your ride. I find it most effective to do this at the posting trot, but it also works at the canter and the walk.

Once you've concluded your ride for the day, praise the horse and send him on at the trot. Encourage and allow him to stretch his neck forward and down by letting the reins slide through your fingers as you ask him to extend. If you've worked him correctly up to this point, he should follow the contact downward by stretching and relaxing. He should stay balanced and continue to carry himself. If he ignores the looser rein and fails to stretch, if he raises his head, or if he falls onto his forehand and rushes, then you'll know that you need to work more on engaging him and putting him on the aids during your next ride.

Your horse will love this reward and will look forward to it as a pleasant end to the ride. In addition, this exercise strengthens and stretches the muscles over his topline that he needs for a good bascule over a fence.

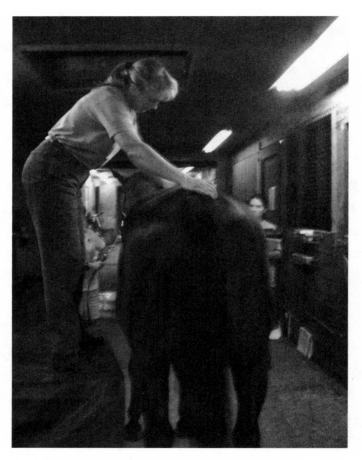

Dr. Angela Erickson-Greco performs a chiropractic adjustment on a horse's sacrum.

tip 51.

When dealing with a sticky training issue, be sure that the horse is physically sound before attempting to fix the problem under saddle. For example, a horse that violently refuses jumps on a regular basis may have a hock problem that makes jumping difficult and painful. Did your mare suddenly develop a bucking habit? Perhaps she's in need of a chiropractic adjustment. Does your horse lean on the reins and try to root them out of your hands? Have his teeth checked. Many owners work not only with a veterinarian, but also with a massage therapist, myotherapist, or chiropractor (or all three).

Once you're sure he's not in pain, then work on training and obedience issues. My trainer used to say (speaking metaphorically, of course) about a slowpoke we were working with, "First, we have him vetted to make sure there's nothing wrong. Then we set his tail on fire."

Elevated poles strengthen a horse's hind end by causing him to step higher with each stride. (These poles look crooked due to the angle of the camera, but they are actually parallel.)

tip 52. Both to keep flatwork interesting

and to strengthen the horse's hindquarters, nothing beats ground poles. Once your horse is happily working over a series of four trotting poles, you can up the ante with a set of elevated poles. Use a jump standard or block to lift the right side of the second rail in your line of trotting poles about a foot off the ground, so it looks like half of a very small crossrail. Then use another standard or block to lift the left side of the third pole in the series. Trot on through, treating the elevated poles just the same as flat poles. Ride them either posting or in your half-seat. Be prepared for an overreaction the first time you try—from a distance, the elevated poles look like a small crossrail, and some horses may try to jump through them. Just stay steady and balanced, half-halting if you need to as you approach the poles, and let the horse figure it out.

Elevated pinwheel poles encourage impulsion . . .

tip 53. Pinwheel poles, the next step up

after elevated poles, combine the value of the elevated poles with a bending line.

Set up a series of four poles in a pinwheel shape, so that they all meet at one end and fan out to 3 feet apart at the other end. Use a block to elevate the innermost ends of the poles (see the

. . . and suspension on a bending line.

photo on the previous page). Pick up a nice, forward posting trot and trot a 20-meter circle around the outside of the poles, not going over them yet. Continue to circle until you think the horse has a solid, true bend. Then attempt the pinwheel poles, aiming for the center of the first pole. Continue to ride forward, looking up and around the circle while using your outside aids to hold the horse in the bend.

You have to ride the bending line correctly, or the exercise won't work, which makes it a great test of a true bend. It's easy to know when you've made a mistake. If you're just pulling the horse's head to one side, rather than bending his whole body around your inside leg with your outside leg and hand, he'll easily escape the poles by popping his outside shoulder and running out. The horse may "die" in the middle of the poles—meaning you didn't have enough impulsion coming into the exercise, or didn't maintain it well. Or, he may fall to the outside and miss the final two poles altogether, meaning that you weren't holding him in a true bend. Keep at it until you get it.

"A horse gallops with its lungs, perseveres with its heart, and wins with its character."

—Federico Tesio

Preparing in advance allows you to focus on riding (and winning!) on show day.

tip 54.
Make a checklist of everything you need for a show, from the tips of your toes to the top of your head, starting with nylon socks to help your boots slide on and ending with bobby pins to keep your hair under your helmet. Make another list for your horse, from the tips of his hooves to the tips of his ears, starting with hoof polish and ending with a cordless trimmer for last-minute touch-ups. Make this list at least a week in advance of the event, so you'll have time to think of anything you might have forgotten. The night before you leave for the show, pack all your gear into the truck and trailer and stock the trailer with hay, water, and bedding. This forethought will avoid unnecessary stress in the morning.

A groom's tote with all the essentials: Fly spray, ShowSheen, water bottle, sweat scraper, brush, hoofpick, and sun hat.

tip 55. Grooms should keep a tote at the ringside with:

Hard brush

Soft brush

Hoof pick

Hoof oil

Several rags, some damp and some dry

ShowSheen

Fly spray

Water bottles

Energy bars

Caulk tools

Sunscreen

Be sure to bring two pairs of comfortable shoes to the show—one pair will inevitably get soaking wet when you bathe the horses. Stay hydrated and wear sunscreen and a baseball cap to protect your face.

A light gray coat is an elegant choice for a rider with a graceful figure and good upper body position.

tip 56.

Although a respectable judge will not mark you down for wearing the wrong color shirt or the wrong brand of helmet, make sure you look neat and workmanlike in the show ring. Don't get too worked up about what's "in" this season in terms of fashion. Clothes should simply match, fit well, and be clean. If you've grown a little too big for last year's britches, invest in a new pair. On a similar note, if your figure or position are slightly less than perfect, light-colored jackets (such as light gray) and plaids accentuate those flaws when they wrinkle in the wrong places. Dark colors and herringbone weaves hide figure flaws better.

tip 57.

Extremely long, thick hair is hard to hide under a helmet. In fact, it's dangerous, because it can change the fit of the helmet, compromising head protection in the event of a fall. Braid your long hair tightly, roll the braid up, and tuck it into a hairnet that comes with a barrette to secure it to the base of the braid, just below your helmet. For very thick hair that won't fit into one of these barretted hairnets, make two braids, pigtail-style, and tuck each one into its own net. It won't look perfect, but it's better than your helmet hovering dangerously above your head atop a pile of hair.

tip 58.

Bring lunch to the show. You need to eat to stay strong and focused. People who skip a meal end up weak and shaky, even if they don't realize it. Typical food at horse shows is of notoriously bad quality—usually something greasy and non-nutritious, like hamburgers and soda that will only weigh you down or even make you feel ill. And it's expensive, too.

As part of your pre-show preparation the night before, pack a cooler with food that's healthy and easy to eat on the go. Turkey or cheese sandwiches on wheat bread, apples, bananas, juice, and bottled water are all good choices. Granola bars or energy bars are perfect when you're too nervous to eat "real" food, or when you just don't have time to stop and eat lunch. On a hot day, salty snacks such as nuts or chips replenish the sodium lost through sweating.

Also pack a bottle of waterless hand sanitizer so you can eat with clean hands. And despite an early departure time, never skip breakfast on a horse-show day.

tip 59. When stabling overnight at the

show, do a stall inspection before putting your horse in the stall. Check for broken or loose boards, loose nails, broken brackets, dirty buckets, bent bars, broken windows, uneven flooring, and damaged locks or hinges on the doors. Ask the show management to resolve any problems that might threaten your horse's safety.

Be careful to keep a safe distance from other riders in the warm-up.

tip 60.

Crowded warm-up or schooling arenas at shows can be hazardous and nerve-wracking. To ensure the safest and least-enervating experience for yourself, your horse, and your fellow competitors, keep a sharp eye out and follow the accepted warm-up ring etiquette.

- When passing someone who's traveling in the opposite direction, pass left shoulder to left shoulder (that is, the rider tracking left—or counterclockwise—stays on the rail, while the rider tracking right moves to the inside).

- If you choose to violate this rule for any reason, clearly and promptly call out "Rail" or "Inside" to indicate on which side of the oncoming rider you will be passing. (An example of a reason to do this might be if you are cantering on the right lead and need to stay on the rail to make a good turn toward a jump. Call out "Rail" to ask another rider to yield the rail to you.) Calling for the rail when you don't really need it is considered rude.

- When passing a slower-moving rider traveling in the same direction, always pass on the inside and announce your presence as you approach by calling, "Passing, inside."

- Riders moving at a faster gait have priority. For example, if you are walking your horse and see that you will soon cross paths with a rider who is cantering toward you, it is your responsibility to yield to the cantering horse. Always give way to a rider who is jumping a fence.

- When jumping, loudly call out the fence you are about to approach. Most warm-ups have at least three fences—a crossrail, a vertical, and an oxer—so simply call out the name of the fence to warn other riders to clear the way.

- If your horse is excessively boisterous and you can't control him, dismount and leave the warm-up as a courtesy to fellow riders. Find a quiet place to longe him until he is safe to ride in company.

tip 61.

When walking a course, make note of any areas of terrain that are uphill, downhill, or have bad footing. An uphill line with normal striding means you'll have to press a bit to make the distance because the hill, even a slight one, will compress your horse's stride. Similarly, slick or muddy footing will cause your horse to shorten his stride. A downhill line naturally lengthens the horse's stride a bit, so you'll have to steady to hit the distance by sitting up and half-halting after the first fence.

tip 62.

When you're allowed to choose your order of go in an over-fences class, never try to go first. You'll want to watch the riders on course before your trip. After walking the course, you'll have a chance to analyze how the lines really ride, and how the distances are working. Does one corner look especially tight? Will you need to ride forward to make the five-stride line? Are horses spooking at the woman in the hat along the rail?

Take these factors into consideration, but in a positive way. Rather than observing the mistakes of others and fearing the worst, plan ahead to make sure you can outride the trouble spots.

Bonus tip: Studying the course in this way also gives you an opportunity to see where you can demonstrate your strong points, as Anne Kursinski recommends: "Look for places on course where you can show off your strong points—be a little more brilliant. . . . Try to figure out all the options the designer has given you at each fence— the showy route, the conservative route—and figure out which one will best suit your horse and you."

---

tip 63. Don't stop riding! No matter what

happens during a class, keep your focus and continue to ride. If you ride a flawless line and you just *know* you nailed it, don't let the joy distract you from your next fence. If you pick up the wrong lead in a hack, don't give up on the class completely—forget about the bad moment and finish up the class respectably. At worst, you'll know you rode well except for the error. At best, it's possible that the judge didn't see the mistake, and since you finished the class well, you'll still pin.

Whatever you do, don't advertise the problem by becoming visibly frustrated or upset. If you pick up the wrong lead, don't look down, grimace, yank the horse back to a trot, and boot him into a canter. What judge wouldn't notice that display? Instead, keep your head and eyes up and your poker face on, while quietly and calmly fixing the problem without a fuss. Becoming angry at your horse in the show ring is not only counterproductive in terms of winning, but it also makes you look bad. Judges remember such behavior.

Use your entrance to highlight your horse's best gait.

tip 64.

You and your horse are being judged from the moment you enter the ring in an equitation or hunter over-fences class. Use your entrance to highlight your, or your horse's, best attributes—first impressions are important. Do you have a really stellar sitting trot? Then trot in that way and let the judge get a good look at you before starting your canter circle. Does your hunter have a relaxed, ground-covering walk? Then walk in and show it off a bit. On the other hand, avoid the aspects of your ride you are least proud of. A hunter with a lot of knee action at the trot should walk in. If you know your canter departure from a walk will be a scramble, do yourself a favor and trot in.

The same applies to your exit. At the end of the course, don't just quit riding and let the horse die, or haul on his mouth to bring him back to an abrupt trot. Finish with a nice, balanced, round circle and a quiet transition. If your horse is a bit strong, try to be subtle about your half-halts. If he is quiet, show it off by letting him leave the ring on a loose rein.

Light seat, light hand, and forward pony are the recipe for a good trot.

tip 65.

In a hunter under-saddle class, don't be afraid to send the horse forward. A horse that's striding out and moving forward is showing off his gaits to his best advantage. Keep your seat light to free his back and let him swing his shoulders. A well-balanced horse should be able to go on a soft (although not loopy) contact and move forward without falling onto his forehand. If he gets heavy or rushes on a light contact, go home and practice your flatwork! Ideally, your aids should be as minimal as possible—invisible to an observer. Don't restrict the horse with a tight rein and heavy seat. Think light, easy, flowing, and forward.

Get comfortable schooling over 3'9" at home before showing at 3'6".

tip 66.

Before making a move up to a higher division at shows, be comfortable and confident jumping the new height (and higher) at home. To prepare to move up from 3' to 3'6" hunters, school regularly over 3'9" at home. When you get into the show ring, the 3'6" fences will look small. By the same token, here's some sports psychology: When you arrive at the show, watch classes that are bigger than yours. Spend the morning watching the Amateur/Owner hunters—and your 3' Modified Adult class in the afternoon will look like a piece of cake.

An additional benefit to schooling at home over higher fences is that you'll learn your horse's limitations. Horse people often note that there are many good 3' horses, but relatively few are physically capable of competing at 3'6". Winning at a certain level is not necessarily a license to move up. Avoid overfacing your horse by challenging him at home, not at a show.

Marty is using an automatic release here, keeping a straight line from bit to elbow rather than resting her hands on the horse's crest.

tip 67.

In an equitation class, choose the more difficult or complex option *only* if you know you can do it well. For example, in a flat class, when the judge calls for you to reverse direction at the walk, you can simply walk a small half circle and return to the rail, or you can perform a turn on the haunches. The turn on the haunches will earn you "bonus points" with the judge, but only if it is well executed. A sloppy turn on the haunches is worse than a graceful half circle.

Although it's rarely seen in the modern equitation ring, a knowledgeable judge will favor the rider who can demonstrate a good automatic release (also called a *following hand*) over fences. But if you have any doubts about your ability to use this advanced release correctly, play it safe and stick to the more basic crest release.

Some judges prefer a hunter to be in a rounder, more collected frame.

tip 68.

If you have time, watch three or four classes ahead of your own. Try to "judge" the riders, assigning them placings based on your own observations. Then listen when the classes are pinned and compare your results. If you were way off, contemplate what the judges' criteria may have been. You'll get a better sense of what a good rider does right, you'll learn what mistakes are most costly, and you'll develop your eye for a nice horse.

Bonus tip: A more sophisticated rider can use this technique to discover what the judge is looking for and apply it to her own ride later that day. For example, does the judge seem to prefer a quiet horse that goes around with a loop in the rein, or does she favor a horse that's on the bit and forward? Which part of the ring does she usually watch in the flat classes? Remember, and make any necessary corrections behind the judge's back, so your horse is going well when you're in her line of sight.

In a crowded flat class, have a plan for negotiating the obstacle course of jumps in the ring.

tip 69.

When competing in a crowded flat class in a ring full of jumps, go into the ring early to scope out possible trouble spots—such as a tight squeeze between two fences where a bottleneck might occur—as well as identifying good lines of travel between the fences. Knowing where the fences are will help you avoid collisions or near-misses with other riders. Plot a route that will keep you in the judge's line of sight as much as possible. Look for open spaces where you can circle if needed. Decide ahead of time whether you want to ride to the outside or the inside of the jumps. Using the ring well will show the judge you know what you're doing, and, equally important, will keep you safe.

Bonus tip: During the class, if you find yourself catching up to a competitor and can't find a spot to circle or pass, ride deep into the corners to add a few strides between your horse and hers.

tip 70.
When asked to perform a counter-canter in an equitation flat test, unless you are very sure of your horse's ability to maintain his balance and hold his lead, make your track around the ring an oval shape rather than a square. Round off the corners and don't ride deep into the turns. Deep corners, which are an invitation to the horse to change his lead, will make you work much harder at trying to maintain the correct bend. An oval-shaped track will also help you maintain a consistent, steady rhythm since you won't have to slow down to balance in the corners.

tip 71.

In under-saddle classes, don't leap into a transition the moment you hear the announcer say, "Canter, please—all canter." Take a moment to prepare your transitions, whether upward or downward. A subtle half-halt, if you need one, will rebalance your horse and let him know that the transition is coming. Flex him to the inside to make sure you get the correct lead. Taking an extra two or three seconds to prepare for a smooth, balanced transition is far better than asking instantly and getting a sloppy, downhill, or rushy change.

Friends on the ground can run errands for you once you're in the saddle.

tip 72. Whenever you show without your

trainer, bring along a knowledgeable friend who can act as groom, horse-holder, jump-setter in the warm-up, coach, and moral supporter. This person will be responsible for everything from running back to the trailer to grab the gloves you forgot to coaching you on your position and pace as you school over fences. A groom/ground person allows you to relax and focus on showing, secure in the knowledge that everything is being taken care of for you. In addition, if you or your horse are injured, it's vital to have someone at the show who knows you and your horse.

After a difficult round, a friend can help you focus on the next class.

tip 73. Learning from your mistakes is

good, but a horse show is not the place to put this aphorism into practice. Put a bad class behind you when you have another coming up, so you can focus on what's happening now, not what happened twenty minutes ago. Instead of dwelling on the mistakes of your previous round, think of the class at hand as a completely new opportunity to show off your strengths. If your horse was too fresh in the earlier class, be confident that he has now gotten it out of his system and is ready to work. If you missed every distance in your first hunter trip, just concentrate on riding your best in the second trip, and chances are that you'll nail the distances.

C. J. and Taz take advantage of a shade tree between classes.

tip 74.

When showing in the summer, your horse needs your help to stay cool. Several steps will reduce the risk of heat exhaustion in weather over 80 degrees Fahrenheit.

Before the show weekend, consider body-clipping the horse if you know it's going to be especially hot. The morning of the show, administer a dose of electrolyte gel to boost the levels of potassium, magnesium, and sodium he'll lose through sweating. During the show, offer the horse a drink as often as possible, but never let him drink more than half a bucket of cold water at one time; too much water can shock his system if he is overheated. Keep two buckets of cool water near the warm-up and showing arenas if your trailer or stall is far away: one for drinking and one for sponging the horse's neck, chest, and between his front and hind legs.

During long breaks between classes, remove the saddle and bridle and give the horse a full hose-down, scrape him dry, and find a shady place to hand-walk him. It's best not to let him stand still for too long, especially if he's going to be working again that day; hand-walking promotes circulation, which helps keep a horse cool. If there isn't any shade to be found, use a white fly sheet to deflect sun off the horse.

Use your opening circle to send the horse up in front of your leg.

tip 75.

A common mistake in the hunter ring is riding with too little pace and impulsion to the first fence. This may be because riders, anticipating an increase of pace throughout the course, try to moderate their speed at the outset. In addition, the first fence is usually set going away from the in gate, which encourages horses to slow down. The result is that riders arrive at the first fence with a long distance and not enough impulsion to make a good effort.

To counteract this problem, use your opening circle to increase pace, sending the horse up in front of your leg with each stride. Build impulsion to the point that you feel you actually have a little *too much* pace. This will set you up nicely for the first line away from the in gate. With a powerful first fence, you'll be able to steady, instead of driving the horse through the first line, helping to offset the natural tendency to speed up throughout the course.

"A horse is a thing of such **beauty**... none will tire of looking at him as long as he displays himself in his **splendor**."

—Xenophon, 400 BC

With such a wide variety of saddles available, it's important to find one that fits you and your horse well. (Caroline Dowd)

tip 76.

Your horse can't perform his best if his saddle is causing him pain by pinching or rubbing. A horse's body changes constantly as he gains or loses muscle and fat. Many horses are thin in the winter and rotund in the summer, so check the fit of your saddle every six months, or anytime you sense that your horse's back is sore.

Without a saddle pad, place your saddle on your horse's back high up on his withers, and then slide it back until it stops naturally. Put two fingers vertically on the pommel. The top of your fingers should be level with the top of the cantle, and the seat of the saddle should be level. Now slide your hand into the gullet at the withers. You should be able to fit three fingers vertically between the withers and the pommel. If the pommel is too low and the cantle too high based on these tests, the tree is too wide. A high pommel and low cantle mean the tree is too narrow.

tip 77.

Many of us ride at home in an old, well-loved saddle and bridle, wearing jeans, chaps, and paddock boots. That's fine—but remember that when you tack up with your shiny show saddle and don your crisp new breeches and black leather field boots, you'll look great, but everything will feel different. Boots and breeches are often much more slippery than chaps, and your show saddle will not be as well broken-in. Practice riding in your show clothes and tack at home for a week before a show to accustom yourself to the new feeling.

tip 78.

ShowSheen and other silicone-based sprays add shine to a coat and prevent dust from sticking to the horse. But never spray these products on your horse's neck or mane before an over-fences class. It's very slippery, and when you try to do a crest release, you'll slip right down the horse's neck. Once during my early riding career when my jumping position was still unstable, I fell off four times in one lesson because I had sprayed ShowSheen on my poor pony's neck. The substance will also rub off onto your reins, making them slippery as well. Don't spray it anywhere near the horse's saddle or girth area either, as it can make the saddle slip.

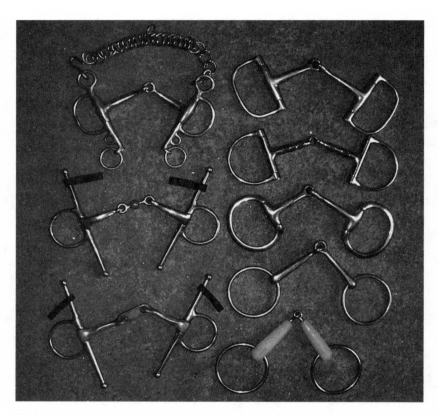

Clockwise from top right: A D-ring, a D-ring with copper rollers, an eggbutt, a loose-ring, a Happy Mouth loose-ring with a plastic mouth, a full-cheek twisted Dr. Bristol with a copper mouth, a double-jointed full-cheek with a copper roller, and a Pelham with a curb chain. All of these bits are snaffles except for the Pelham.

tip 79.

Try different bits. In every good trainer's tack room is a wide range of bits to suit a variety of horses— or even different bits to fit the same horse at varying levels of training. Many riders, for example, school in a plain, gentle snaffle at home but change to a stronger bit—such as a Pelham with a curb chain or a twisted snaffle—for horse shows when they know their horse is going to be stronger. If you're planning to use a different bit at a show, be sure you school in it a few times at home to accustom the horse and yourself to the different feel.

However, an exotic bit will not solve training problems. Many horses end up *over-bitted* when their riders have not properly taught them to respond to seat and leg aids or have not allowed them enough turnout time to "get the bucks out" before riding. The ideal is that all horses should go nicely in a snaffle, at least when schooling at home. But there are many different *kinds* of snaffle bits, including French links, mullen-mouths, full-cheeks, eggbutts, loose-rings, and bits made of different materials, such as plastic, rubber, or copper. None of these bits is inherently harsher or milder than the others, but they each produce a unique feeling for the horse. A full-cheek bit, for example, presses against the sides of the horse's face to help turn his head; it also applies a small amount of poll pressure. A loose-ring snaffle moves freely in the horse's mouth to encourage salivation and discourage leaning.

Experiment with various kinds of snaffles until you find the one that works best for your horse—but remember, in two months, or even two days, he might not be the same horse anymore. Don't hesitate to change bits frequently if you need to.

tip 80.

When bringing a horse with white socks or stockings to a show, clip the stockings a week beforehand to give them time to grow out a bit. When clipped too short, they'll look pink from the skin showing through. Then bathe the horse the day before the show, using a whitening shampoo on his "chrome." When the horse is dry, sprinkle a layer of baby powder or cornstarch onto the markings. If the horse's legs become dirty overnight or in the trailer, brushing off the powder at the show will take the dirt with it, leaving gleaming white socks.

Schooling braids for a schooling show.

tip 81. Always braid your horse's mane

for shows, even schooling shows. Braiding is a difficult art, and the only way to learn to braid well is to practice, practice, practice. A schooling show is an opportunity to practice riding and showing in a casual setting, so use the opportunity to work on your braiding skills as well. At a schooling show, you won't be embarrassed if your horse makes mistakes, so you don't have to be embarrassed if your braids look messy either.

Bonus tip: A mane is much less slippery and therefore easier to braid if you don't use shampoo. During your horse's pre-show bath, use only plain water on the mane or, if it's clean enough, skip washing it altogether.

---

tip 82.
Many horses with under-saddle problems such as head-tossing, pulling, rearing, going behind or above the bit, and generally refusing to accept bit contact are expressing discomfort in their mouths. They may behave much better in a hackamore or bitless bridle, so don't hesitate to experiment with bitless options. If you find that your jumper goes much better in a hackamore, you're in good company; many top-level Grand Prix show jumpers use hackamores.

Show regulations prevent hunters and equitation horses from being shown bitless. Nevertheless, a few weeks of retraining in a bit-

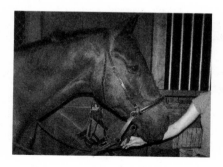

A bitless bridle. The reins connect to cheekpieces that cross under the horse's jaw and turn his head by applying pressure to the opposite side of his face. This patented bridle is available through www.bitlessbridle.com.

less bridle can do wonders for a difficult horse, who can then be changed back to a regular snaffle bridle. For example, my off-the-track Thoroughbred racehorse believed that bit pressure was a signal to go faster, and he often leaned on the bit instead of using his hindquarters to balance himself. I removed the distracting and confusing bit, started using a bitless bridle, and taught him to respond to my steadying seat and leg aids. When I put him back in a snaffle, he was in a much better frame of mind to listen to and accept the bit.

Or you could just skip the bridle altogether. (Courtesy of Sarah Weingarten)

A shiny pony is the result of good daily grooming.

tip 83.

A beautiful, healthy coat can't be faked by a bath and an application of ShowSheen the day before a horse show. To achieve a glowing show-ring shine, you must curry and brush your horse daily to remove dust, dander, and loose hair, as well as to increase circulation to the skin that promotes a healthy coat. Daily grooming also affords you an opportunity to spot developing problems such as swelling or heat in the legs before they become serious.

Bonus tip: Even if you are fortunate enough to board at a stable with grooms to do this work for you, I encourage you to spend some time grooming the horse yourself. Friendly grooming sessions help you develop a relationship with your horse, so that he sees you as a positive part of his life rather than just someone who shows up to make him work. This in turn leads to a more positive and willing attitude when you ride.

A correctly adjusted running martingale on an equitation horse.
(PhelpsPhotos.com)

tip 84.

"As for the running martingale, I would never ride in a show-jumping competition without one," Bill Steinkraus acknowledges in his *Reflections on Riding and Jumping*. A running martingale should be long enough to allow the horse nearly free use of its head and neck, but exert a downward pressure on the bit if the horse raises it higher than his withers. This piece of equipment isn't legal in the hunter divisions, but it is a useful tool for equitation horses or jumpers. "A well-trained horse won't normally bring the martingale into play very often during a round," Steinkraus notes, "but when one's efforts to shorten stride are being resisted and the biggest fence on the course looms, that precious 'nickel's worth' of restraint can make the difference between a clear round and a wreck."

A well-groomed horse, clean tack, and clothes that fit are important in your weekly lessons.

tip 85.

Presentation is important in the show ring, so look for the little details: Does your stirrup leather dangle from the saddle flap? Trim it to lie flush with the flap. Are your bridle's bit rings green and crusty? Scrub and polish them. Is there mud on your boots? Wipe it off. Does your hair stray out from under your hunt cap? Bobby-pin it.

Even during your weekly lessons, looking neat and tidy shows respect for your trainer, your horse, and yourself. Clothes that are baggy, boots that don't fit, hair that is unkempt, and tack that is not cared for are not just unattractive—they can be unsafe. Dried-out stirrup leathers or bridle parts, for example, can break at just the wrong moment, leading to an accident. In addition, loose clothes conceal your arm, hip, and leg positions from your instructor. Even if your trainer doesn't ask you to, tuck in your shirt and comb the shavings from your mount's tail. Cultivating these good habits at home will pay off in the show ring.

"The **knowledge** of the nature of a horse is one of the first foundations of **the art** of riding it, and **every horseman** must make it his principal study."

—François de la Guérinière

tip 86.

Read. You are on the right track already: you are reading this book. Most horse people have large and ever-increasing collections of magazines and books about riding. Take advantage of the vast oceans of knowledge that are out there for the absorbing. Seek out books by authors whose opinions you respect and trust, and read as much as you can (see the Further Reading section for some suggestions). Take the lessons that apply to you from each book, and don't hesitate to let the rest go. Read the newest books and magazine articles, and read the decades-old classics. Study the photographs and analyze the horses' and riders' position and balance. Many good videotapes and DVDs are also available. Watch the parts that interest you over and over again to train your mind's eye to recognize the correct position.

If the cost of building your own library is a concern, think about this: How much would you pay to attend a clinic with your favorite professional rider or trainer? A few hundred dollars? Now think of a book as a clinic tailored just for you, and available for you to attend whenever you need to—and it's only a fraction of the clinic fee. Buy the book. You won't regret it.

tip 87.

Watch great riders. If you can, go to big shows in your area as a spectator. Don't be afraid to approach a rider or trainer during a quiet moment to ask questions about something you saw him or her do in the ring or schooling area. During the winter, when you're stuck indoors, rent videos of top-level shows. Watching and analyzing the style and form of show-jumping giants such as Anne Kursinski, McLain Ward, Meredith Michaels-Beerbaum, Joe Fargis, Rodrigo Pessoa, Beezie Madden, or Margie Goldstein Engle can help you troubleshoot and develop your own jumping form. In addition, you might pick up some useful ideas for negotiating a difficult turn or handling a strong horse.

Participating in a dressage show can help identify weak spots in your training.

tip 88. Diversify your riding experiences.

Don't be a discipline snob; if the opportunity arises to attend a natural horsemanship clinic, take a lesson with a dressage instructor, or ride a friend's Western reining horse, by all means, seize it. The natural horsemanship clinician might help you to better understand and communicate with your horse. The dressage instructor may have some useful advice on improving your half-halts or lateral work. The reiner just may teach you a little something about flying changes.

I tend to twist my upper body to the left when riding. Until I saw this photo, I didn't realize just how severe the problem was.

tip 89.

Ask someone to videotape or photograph your ride. What we feel in the saddle often bears little relationship to reality, and seeing yourself ride can open your eyes to the subtler flaws of your riding. Even if you are already aware of areas that need improvement, watching a videotape can help you more deeply understand the nature of the flaws and, with the help of your trainer, formulate a plan for improvement. On the positive side, our flaws can often feel horrible and embarrassing, when to the observer they are hardly noticeable. Watching your ride on tape can help put such things into perspective.

At designated checkpoints, ask yourself, "Are my elbows in?"

tip 90.

Let's say you are having a specific problem that you are aware of but can't seem to fix. For example, your left wrist always pivots inward, causing your elbow to lock. Your trainer has pointed this out to you many times, yet you just can't seem to break the habit.

Your body has become accustomed to that feeling, so it feels "wrong" to keep your wrist straight. If you consciously make an adjustment, your body "fixes" itself right back to where it feels natural the moment your focus drifts away. So use each dressage letter (A, K, E, H, C, M, B, F) as a "trigger" that causes you to become aware of your left wrist. If your arena doesn't have letters, use the four corners of the ring plus a point halfway down each long side. As you pass each checkpoint, ask yourself, "Is my wrist straight?" If not, then fix it. At the next letter, check again. During your next ride, use only every other checkpoint, until eventually, you'll use only one checkpoint.

By using convenient visual cues to bring your focus back to where you need it to be, you can quickly relearn correct positions. Once your wrist is straightened, use the trigger method on another errant body part, such as "Are my eyes up?" or "Are my shoulders back?"

Alyssa and Cinnamon's first schooling show is the first step in a lifetime of successful showing.

tip 91. Keep goals achievable. Presenting

yourself and your horse with a task that is too difficult sets you up for failure and disappointment. Keep things positive by breaking both your short- and long-term goals into achievable segments. For example, your goal is to learn to leg-yield from the centerline to the rail at the trot. Your first goal is to learn to leg-yield one step at a walk. This sounds silly, but take this first step seriously. If you can't take one perfect lateral step at a walk, your trotting leg-yields will be sloppy at best.

Take a similar approach to long-term goals. If you want to win a year-end award on the A circuit, your first goal will be stepping into the ring for your first class, confidently and calmly. A friend who is a sixty-year-old beginning dressage rider announced last year that her goal for the season was to "trot straight down the centerline and halt at X," which is the first movement of the Introductory-level dressage test. "After that," she said, "I don't care what happens!" Setting her sights on this humble goal gave her the motivation and confidence to attend her first show. After achieving a flawless halt at X, she had achieved her main goal, which freed her to relax and ride the rest of an excellent test.

With his snappy knees, this flashy hunter won't be flipping over any fences.

tip 92.

For a long time I believed that the judging of hunter style over fences was based only on attractiveness—a horse with a nice bascule and a snappy front end is prettier to look at than one that jumps hollow with dangling legs. I later learned that the underlying elements of good hunter form are actually based on safety. For example, a horse that hangs a leg is likely to catch it in a jump and flip over. A horse that is heavy on the forehand may stumble. That is to say, the most heavily penalized flaws in a hunter are the ones that make him unsafe to ride over a course.

This knowledge helped me to conceptualize the training and showing of hunters and made me much more respectful of the division. Learn the logic behind the judging of your classes, and you will be much better able to recognize a quality animal, train your horse to its best advantage, and follow the placings at shows.

tip 93.

When you step into the show ring, be prepared to handle any setbacks that may occur. However, it is equally important not to focus on negative ideas, which can detract from your ride. "In riding," says Anne Kursinski, "there's a fine line between awareness and overreaction—between having a solution ready in case a problem arises and anticipating the problem so much that you may actually trigger it."

A situation seen at nearly every show is the rider who is so afraid that her mount may act up that the horse feels the rider's tension and becomes nervous. The horse then fulfills the rider's fears by spooking or bolting in the ring. Instead of concentrating on what your horse may do wrong, be confident that he will behave, while knowing that if anything untoward does happen, you will be relaxed and ready to respond correctly.

tip 94.

In 2004 I attended the Ox Ridge charity show to watch the Grand Prix jumpers. One line on the jump-off course was particularly awkward—riders had to jump the first fence of a tight combination, then sharply turn right to jump a fence that was on a different line. Several horses were startled by this because they expected to be asked to jump the second fence in the combination rather than turning. One clever rider entered the ring and, before crossing the start line to begin his trip, galloped toward the first of these fences and halted just in front of it. Then during their round, this pair made a smooth, tight turn after the first fence because the horse remembered the halt and was waiting for the rider's aids to tell him what to do, rather than locking himself into the line.

Like this rider, think intelligently about the course before entering the jumper ring, and plan a strategy to make the awkward spots work for you. Imagine how your horse sees the course, and use that insight to your advantage.

Maintain your focus while on course.

tip 95.

Some riders have trouble focusing while in the show ring. They are distracted by the sight of friends along the rail, thoughts of winning, fears of losing, or memories of past events. "If you catch your mind straying on course," advises Anne Kursinski, "bring it back to the things you know make you ride successfully at home: position, pace, rhythm, line." To achieve this goal, develop a mantra that you can recite silently to keep your mind in the game. This mantra may be different for each rider. One may repeat *Shoulders back, eyes up*, while another recites, *Rhythm and straight*, and still another simply counts strides the entire way around the course. "Do whatever you can to reach back to the simple techniques you've used in schooling to keep your mind present and on the job," Kursinski says.

tip 96. Use visualization techniques in

your riding. Visualization is useful because images speak directly to your body and your senses, bypassing complicated verbalization that can often be imprecise, confusing, or distracting. For example, instead of thinking "Let my shoulders, back, and knees relax while I soften into the saddle and let my hips and seat follow the swinging motion of the horse's back," simply imagine, "Melt." See how much simpler that is?

My personal favorite image, described by Sally Swift in her classic book, *Centered Riding,* is that of your belt buckle tied to a point in the sky out in front of you. As you ride, imagine that your buckle is being pulled forward by the string. This puts your hips, chest, and shoulders in the right alignment without creating the tension that comes from trying to forcefully pull your shoulders back and down.

Another of Sally Swift's visual tools is to visualize yourself as a tree, with the trunk growing up out of the saddle toward the sky while the roots stretch down around the horse and toward the ground. If these images don't help you, find others that will— *Centered Riding* is full of them, as are Jane Savoie's books.

tip 97. As a way to further your understanding of striding, course mechanics, and the fundamentals of course design, volunteer to serve on the jump crew at a show. As the jump crew sets the fences for each class, you'll have a hands-on lesson about how striding is measured for the varying classes, divisions, and heights, and you'll get an inside look at how course designers decide what questions to ask of the riders and horses. Pay close attention to the course designer, and ask questions during quiet moments while he or she is not busy setting the course.

tip 98.
When you are paralyzed at a show by a fear of embarrassment, remember that your coach, friends, and family are there to support you, not to criticize you. In addition, your competitors are probably too concerned with their own rides to worry about what may happen during yours. I once had a hunter round in which my horse pretty much flew around the course at a flat-out gallop, while I found myself unable to slow him down. We did finish the course, but I left the ring in tears of humiliation—certainly no *good* rider would have allowed her horse to race in such an undignified way.

To my surprise, however, not only my mom but even my trainer and my competitors were impressed by the fact that I had actually finished the round and jumped every fence without a crash. One of the other riders from the class approached me and said, "Wow, you're really brave. I could never ride a horse like that." She wasn't laughing at me at all.

tip 99.

Keep a riding journal in which you take notes after each ride. Note any progress you've made, new things you've learned, changes in your horse's attitude, or goals for the next ride. Your journal will help you focus on what you want to achieve with your horse and will also remind you of just how far you've come. When you're frustrated after an awful ride, flip back a few months in your journal to read about those weeks when you were battling through a bucking phase. Or read about how proud you were last year when you first cantered without stirrups. You'll feel much better realizing the progress you've made since then.

Good equitation means good riding.

tip 100. Understand the function be-

hind the form of equitation. Good riding is not, as equitation is so often described, simply "looking pretty" on a horse. There is solid reasoning behind all the "rules" of horsemanship, and understanding these reasons will help you to become a more effective rider rather than a model on horseback. For example, keeping your back flat and shoulders back over fences not only looks much prettier than hunching up, but it also keeps your head and eyes up and looking where you're going, keeps your balance back over your heels, allows your arms and hands to follow the horse's mouth accurately, and helps you balance on landing. Knowing such things allows you to see the interconnectedness of your body parts and to understand how and why each part affects all the other parts. This in turn helps you become a more balanced and competent rider, and hence, a prettier equitation competitor.

tip 101.

Very few unmounted activities use the same muscle groups as riding. Even a very fit biker or runner will be sore after a ride on a horse. The best activities to improve our riding are those that improve overall fitness—yoga or Pilates. With their emphasis on core strength (that is, abdominal and lower back muscles), balance, and flexibility, they develop the same assets that we need as riders. Especially if you can only ride once or twice a week, consider taking up yoga or Pilates to help your equitation. Taking a class once a week is ideal.

If you don't have the time or money to spend on actual classes, books and videos are a good source of instruction. Linda Benedik and Veronica Wirth's *Yoga for Equestrians* illustrates several poses that are useful for riders. Marty Whittle and Nicole Cuomo's *Manual for Mounted Yoga* teaches yoga poses that can be practiced while riding—a great way to have fun while developing balance and flexibility.

Further Reading

Books

Benedik, Linda, and Veronica Wirth. *Yoga for Equestrians*. North Pomfret, Vermont: Trafalgar Square, 2000.

Klimke, Reiner. *Basic Training of the Young Horse*. Guilford, Connecticut: The Lyons Press, 2000.

Kursinski, Anne, with Miranda Lorraine. *Anne Kursinski's Riding and Jumping Clinic*. New York: Doubleday, 1995.

McEvoy, Hallie. *Showing for Beginners*. Guilford, Connecticut: The Lyons Press, 2003.

Morris, George H. *Hunter Seat Equitation, 3rd ed*. Garden City, New York: Doubleday & Company, 1990.

Savoie, Jane. *Cross-Train Your Horse*. North Pomfret, Vermont: Trafalgar Square, 1998.

Steinkraus, William. *Reflections on Riding and Jumping* (Revised and Updated). North Pomfret, Vermont: Trafalgar Square, 1997.

Swift, Sally. *Centered Riding*. North Pomfret, Vermont: Trafalgar Square, 1985.

White-Mullin, Anna Jane. *Judging Hunters and Hunter Seat Equitation*. New York: Arco Publishing, 1984.

White-Mullin, Anna Jane. *Winning*. North Pomfret, Vermont: Trafalgar Square, 1992.

Whittle, Marty, and Nicole Cuomo. *Manual for Mounted Yoga*. Loveland, Colorado: Alpine Publications, forthcoming.

Magazines

The Chronicle of the Horse
P.O. Box 46
Middleburg, VA 20118
(540) 687-6341
www.chronofhorse.com

Equestrian

West of the Mississippi:
Kim Russell
(859) 225-6938
krussell@usef.org
www.usef.org

East of the Mississippi:
Crissi White
(859) 225-6936
cwhite@usef.org

Practical Horseman
Primedia Equine Network
656 Quince Orchard Road
Suite 600
Gaithersburg, MD 20878
www.equisearch.com

Websites

www.ahjf.org

The official site of the American Hunter/Jumper Foundation.

www.chronicleforums.com

The *Chronicle of the Horse* bulletin board forums, where horse people of various disciplines meet to discuss topics of mutual concern.

www.horsecity.com

An excellent source for all kinds of horse-related information, from tack and training to health and safety.

www.equisearch.com

The online portal for *Practical Horseman* and *Equus* magazines, among others.

www.towerheads.com

An online news outlet for the hunter/jumper show scene featuring interviews, reports, results, and photos.

www.usef.org

The official site of the United States Equestrian Federation, the national governing body of equestrian sport. The source for rules and regulations and the latest news on policy changes.

www.uset.com

The official site of the United States Equestrian Team.

www.101horsekeepingtips.com

The website for this book.

Acknowledgments

This book represents the combined knowledge and expertise of the many capable horsemen and -women I've worked with throughout my life. Credit goes to all of them. In particular, I thank Mott Atherholt and Caroline Dowd for giving me my start in the horse world and for teaching me from the very beginning to be a good horseman as well as a rider. Thanks to Marty Whittle at Top Cat Farm in Killingworth, Connecticut, for expanding my horse horizons and helping me find George. Marty and her Dutch Warmblood/Clydesdale cross jumper, Teddy, are the models for many of the photos in this book. Thanks to Jennifer Sisk and Suzanne Mancheski at Crystal Wood Stables in Durham, Connecticut, for reading the manuscript and for "being there." Thanks to all the riders at Crystal Wood who let me follow them around with my camera at horse shows—Suzanne, Patty, Noreen, Melissa, Alyssa, Joy, C. J., Whitney, and Tammy. Thanks to Sarah Weingarten and Cheerio for their photos as well.

This book would also not have come to be without the support and faith of the wonderful people at The Lyons Press. Thanks very much to Steve Price, my intrepid editor and mentor, for wisdom and equanimity, and to Jay Cassell, now at *Field & Stream*, for taking a chance on me.

Thanks to Chris Mongillo, Sheryl Kober, Kirsten Livingston, Ryan Edmonds, Melissa Hayes, Cynthia Goss, Anne Jones, Theresa Eldredge, and Kathryn Mennone, who have all helped to make this book and this series a sucess.

Last but not least, thanks to my family, especially my husband Jason for his support, patience, and camerawork.